The
★ ★
UNITED
STATES
PRESIDENTS

Herbert
HOOVER

BreAnn Rumsch

Big Buddy Books
An Imprint of Abdo Publishing
abdopublishing.com

abdopublishing.com

Printed in the United States of America, North Mankato, Minnesota
062016
092016

 THIS BOOK CONTAINS
RECYCLED MATERIALS

Design: Sarah DeYoung, Mighty Media, Inc.
Production: Mighty Media, Inc.
Editor: Lauren Kukla
Cover Photograph: Getty Images
Interior Photographs: AP Images (pp. 5, 11, 13, 17, 23); Corbis (pp. 21, 27, 29); Getty Images (pp. 7, 25);
     Library of Congress (pp. 6, 15, 19); National Park Service (pp. 7, 9)

Cataloging-in-Publication Data

Names: Rumsch, BreAnn, author.
Title: Herbert Hoover / by BreAnn Rumsch.
Description: Minneapolis, MN : Abdo Publishing, [2017] | Series: United States
     presidents | Includes bibliographical references and index.
Identifiers: LCCN 2015957492 | ISBN 9781680781007 (lib. bdg.) |
     ISBN 9781680775204 (ebook)
Subjects: LCSH: Hoover, Herbert, 1874-1964--Juvenile literature. | Presidents--
     United States--Biography--Juvenile literature. | United States--Politics and
     government--1929-1933--Juvenile literature.
Classification: DDC 973.916/092 [B]--dc23
LC record available at http://lccn.loc.gov/2015957492

Contents

Herbert Hoover

Herbert Hoover was the thirty-first US president. He took office in 1928. At the time, the nation's **economy** seemed strong. But in late 1929, it started to fail.

A long period of trouble fell across the United States. This time became known as the **Great Depression**. Many Americans blamed Hoover for their problems.

Still, Hoover continued to work hard for his country. In time, he was recognized for all he did for the United States and the world.

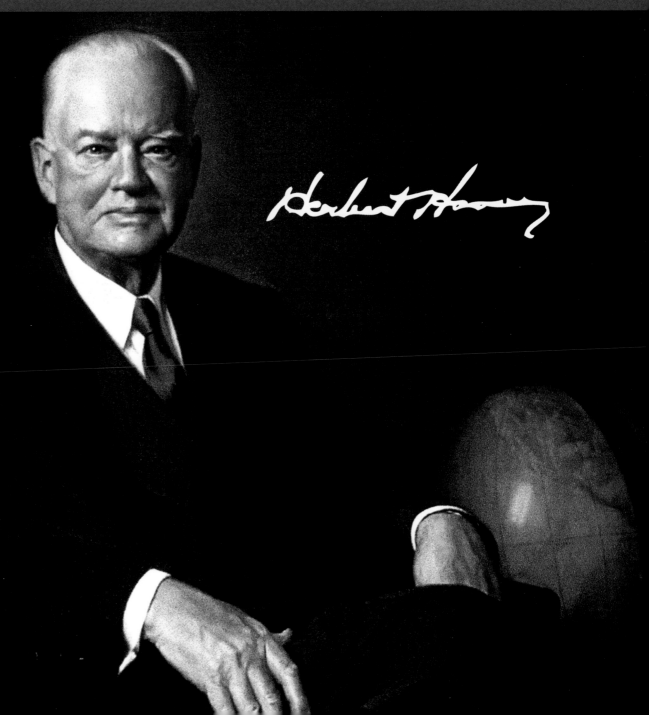

Timeline

1874

On August 10, Herbert Clark Hoover was born in West Branch, Iowa.

1914

World War I began.

1921

Hoover became **secretary of commerce** under President Warren G. Harding.

1929

On March 4, Hoover became the thirty-first president of the United States. The **stock market** crashed in October.

1939

World War II began. Hoover led the Polish **Relief** Commission.

1932

Hoover lost reelection to Franklin D. Roosevelt.

1964

On October 20, Herbert Hoover died.

7

Young Bert

Herbert Clark Hoover was born in West Branch, Iowa, on August 10, 1874. Everyone called him Bert. Bert's parents were Jesse and Hulda Hoover. Sadly, both Bert's parents died when he was a child. So, relatives took in Bert and his brother and sister.

★ FAST FACTS ★

Born: August 10, 1874

Wife: Lou Henry (1874–1944)

Children: two

Political Party: Republican

Age at Inauguration: 54

Years Served: 1929–1933

Vice President: Charles Curtis

Died: October 20, 1964, age 90

Bert's birthplace in West Branch, Iowa. Bert and his family believed in living a simple life, working hard, and helping others.

Studies and Mining

In 1891, Hoover moved to California. There, he studied **geology** at Stanford University. In 1895, Hoover finished school at Stanford. Then, he took a job in a California gold mine.

In 1897, Hoover got a job with Bewick, Moreing & Company. The company sent Hoover to Australia. There, he taught Australians about US mining methods. Hoover also discovered a gold mine. It earned him and the company a great deal of money.

At Stanford, Hoover (*lower left*) belonged to a student group that practiced surveying, or measuring land.

World Traveler

On February 10, 1899, Hoover married Lou Henry. That same day, they boarded a ship to China. There, Hoover helped the Chinese government find coal fields and **minerals**.

In 1903, Hoover and Lou set out on a world journey. By 1908, the Hoovers had settled in London, England. Meanwhile, Hoover and Lou had also welcomed two sons. Hoover was now a wealthy man. He formed his own **engineering** company.

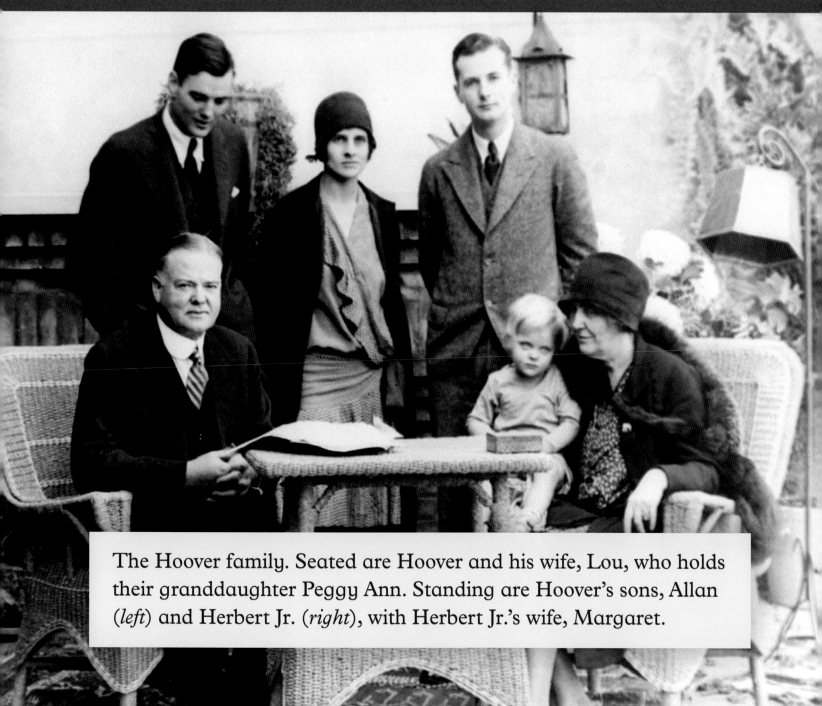

The Hoover family. Seated are Hoover and his wife, Lou, who holds their granddaughter Peggy Ann. Standing are Hoover's sons, Allan (*left*) and Herbert Jr. (*right*), with Herbert Jr.'s wife, Margaret.

World War I

Hoover's new business was a success. However, he wanted to move into public service. Then, **World War I** began in Europe in 1914. In 1917, the United States entered the war.

President Woodrow Wilson asked Hoover to come home. Then Wilson made him the US food **administrator**. The United States needed to have enough food to send to its troops fighting in Europe. So, Hoover asked Americans to limit the food they ate.

About 14 million
US families
followed Hoover's
food program
to save food
for the troops.

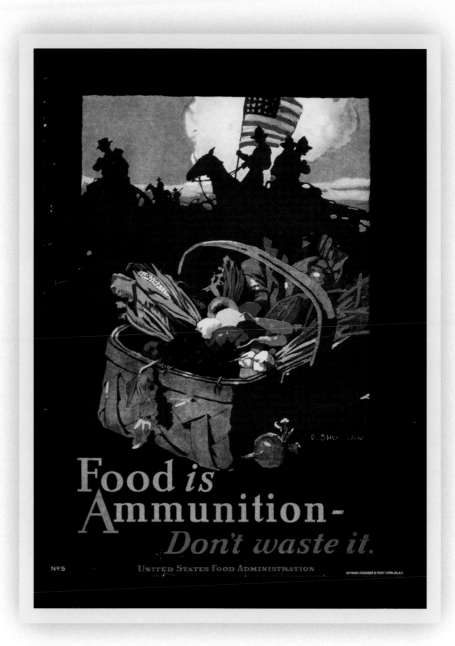

Public Service

Hoover's public service work made him famous. He hoped **Republicans** would choose him to run for president in 1920. However, the Republicans chose Warren G. Harding instead. Harding became the next president.

Hoover became the **secretary of commerce** in 1921. That same year, Hoover planned water and power **developments** along the Colorado River. His ideas eventually led to the building of Hoover Dam.

President Calvin Coolidge (*left*) with Secretary Hoover. Coolidge had been vice president, but he became president when Harding died in 1923.

Meanwhile, Secretary Hoover took on many service projects. In 1923, he started an **organization** to help sick children in need. Then in 1927, the Mississippi River flooded. Hoover quickly organized a **program** for flood **relief**.

Hoover's great works continued to make him popular with Americans. In 1928, the **Republican** Party chose Hoover to run for president. The **Democrats** chose Alfred E. Smith. In the election, voters made Hoover president of the United States.

★ DID YOU KNOW? ★

Hoover was one of two presidents to give away his presidential salary. The other was John F. Kennedy.

Hoover served as president of Better Homes in America throughout the 1920s. This group lowered the cost of new homes.

President Hoover

Hoover took office on March 4, 1929. At the time, the United States was experiencing a period of **economic** success. Hoover wanted Americans to share in the nation's wealth.

Hoover created many new **organizations**. He suggested tax cuts for the poor. He fought for the rights of Native Americans.

The president also suggested a series of dams. He set up more national parks. These projects created many new jobs.

PRESIDENT HOOVER'S CABINET

March 4, 1929–March 4, 1933

★ **STATE:** Henry L. Stimson

★ **TREASURY:** Andrew W. Mellon,
Ogden L. Mills (from February 13, 1932)

★ **WAR:** James W. Good,
Patrick J. Hurley (from December 9, 1929)

★ **NAVY:** Charles Francis Adams

★ **ATTORNEY GENERAL:** William D. Mitchell

★ **INTERIOR:** Ray Lyman Wilbur

★ **AGRICULTURE:** Arthur M. Hyde

★ **COMMERCE:** Robert P. Lamont,
Roy D. Chapin (from December 14, 1932)

★ **LABOR:** James J. Davis,
William N. Doak (from December 9, 1930)

Hoover signed the
Farm Relief Bill
in 1929 to help farmers.

21

Meanwhile, people had been making money in the **stock market**. However, many had borrowed money from banks to buy stocks. As a result, many Americans went into **debt**.

Then, stock prices crashed. Many people could not repay the money they had borrowed. Banks began to suffer. People lost their savings.

Businesses also suffered because people had less money to spend. A **recession** began. Hoover tried to stop it. Yet, the recession turned into the **Great Depression**.

SUPREME COURT APPOINTMENTS

Charles Evans Hughes: 1930

Owen Roberts: 1930

Benjamin Nathan Cardozo: 1932

The stock market crash on October 24, 1929, was the worst financial upset in US history. The day became known as Black Thursday.

Troubled Times

President Hoover worked hard to help the country out of the **Great Depression**. He created government **programs** that would create more jobs for people. Still, families across the nation were homeless.

In 1932, Hoover was up for reelection. He ran against New York governor Franklin D. Roosevelt. Many Americans blamed Hoover for the Great Depression. So, Roosevelt easily won the election. But the Great Depression would not end until 1942.

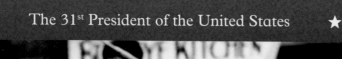

All over the country, homeless people built shack communities. These were called Hoovervilles.

Later Life

The Hoovers left the White House in March 1933. But Hoover stayed busy. He continued to help people.

In 1939, **World War II** began when Germany attacked Poland. Hoover led the Polish **Relief** Commission. The **organization** provided food for thousands of Polish children during the war.

World War II ended in 1945. It had caused food shortages across Europe. In 1946, Hoover directed a group that helped feed millions of Europeans.

Hoover traveled to nearly 40 countries in 1946. While in Poland, he visited children who had lost their parents.

Hoover spent the rest of his days writing, giving speeches, and advising US presidents. By 1963, Hoover had grown ill. On October 20, 1964, he died.

Herbert Hoover was known as a great problem solver. But he faced a **challenging** presidency. Americans blamed him for the **Great Depression**. Yet, later in life, Hoover earned America's respect for his hard work.

★ DID YOU KNOW? ★

Hoover loved the outdoors. He especially enjoyed fishing. He even wrote a book about this favorite hobby called *Fishing for Fun*.

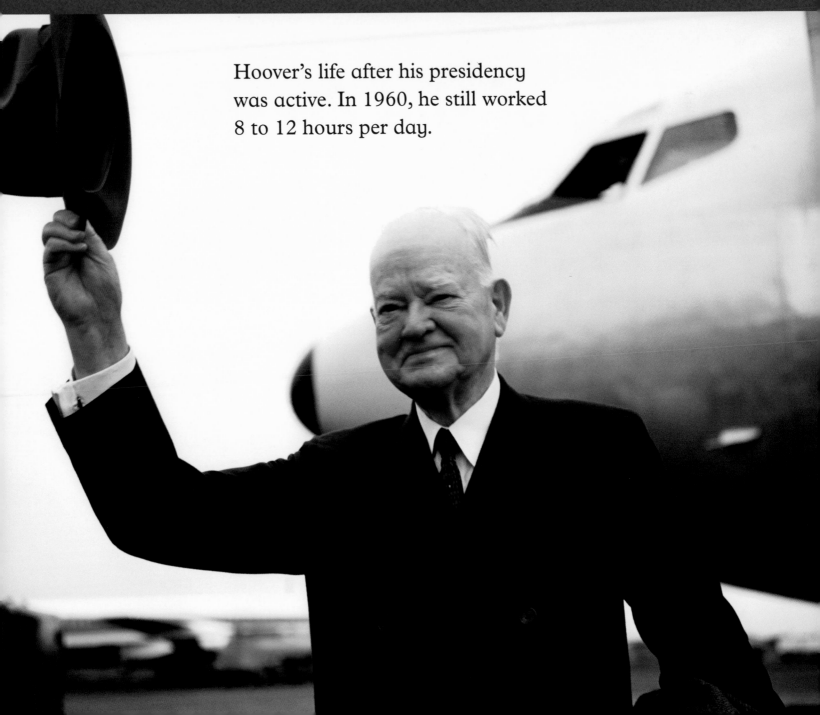

Hoover's life after his presidency was active. In 1960, he still worked 8 to 12 hours per day.

Office of the President

Branches of Government

The US government has three branches. They are the executive, legislative, and judicial branches. Each branch has some power over the others. This is called a system of checks and balances.

★ **Executive Branch**

The executive branch enforces laws. It is made up of the president, the vice president, and the president's cabinet. The president represents the United States around the world. He or she also signs bills into law and leads the military.

★ **Legislative Branch**

The legislative branch makes laws, maintains the military, and regulates trade. It also has the power to declare war. This branch includes the Senate and the House of Representatives. Together, these two houses form Congress.

★ **Judicial Branch**

The judicial branch interprets laws. It is made up of district courts, courts of appeals, and the Supreme Court. District courts try cases. Sometimes people disagree with a trial's outcome. Then he or she may appeal. If a court of appeals supports the ruling, a person may appeal to the Supreme Court.

Qualifications for Office

To be president, a candidate must be at least 35 years old. The person must be a natural-born US citizen. He or she must also have lived in the United States for at least 14 years.

Electoral College

The US presidential election is an indirect election. Voters from each state choose electors. These electors represent their state in the Electoral College. Each elector has one electoral vote. Electors cast their vote for the candidate with the highest number of votes from people in their state. A candidate must receive the majority of Electoral College votes to win.

Term of Office

Each president may be elected to two four-year terms. The presidential election is held on the Tuesday after the first Monday in November. The president is sworn in on January 20 of the following year. At that time, he or she takes the oath of office.
It states:

> I do solemnly swear (or affirm) that I will faithfully execute the office of President of the United States, and will to the best of my ability, preserve, protect and defend the Constitution of the United States.

31

Line of Succession

The Presidential Succession Act of 1947 states who becomes president if the president cannot serve. The vice president is first in the line. Next are the Speaker of the House and the President Pro Tempore of the Senate. It may happen that none of these individuals is able to serve. Then the office falls to the president's cabinet members. They would take office in the order in which each department was created:

Secretary of State

Secretary of the Treasury

Secretary of Defense

Attorney General

Secretary of the Interior

Secretary of Agriculture

Secretary of Commerce

Secretary of Labor

Secretary of Health and Human Services

Secretary of Housing and Urban Development

Secretary of Transportation

Secretary of Energy

Secretary of Education

Secretary of Veterans Affairs

Secretary of Homeland Security

Benefits

★ While in office, the president receives a salary. It is $400,000 per year. He or she lives in the White House. The president also has 24-hour Secret Service protection.

★ The president may travel on a Boeing 747 jet. This special jet is called Air Force One. It can hold 70 passengers. It has kitchens, a dining room, sleeping areas, and more. Air Force One can fly halfway around the world before needing to refuel. It can even refuel in flight!

★ When the president travels by car, he or she uses Cadillac One. It is a Cadillac Deville that has been modified. The car has heavy armor and communications systems. The president may even take Cadillac One along when visiting other countries.

★ The president also travels on a helicopter. It is called Marine One. It may also be taken along when the president visits other countries.

★ Sometimes the president needs to get away with family and friends. Camp David is the official presidential retreat. It is located in Maryland. The US Navy maintains the retreat. The US Marine Corps keeps it secure. The camp offers swimming, tennis, golf, and hiking.

★ When the president leaves office, he or she receives lifetime Secret Service protection. He or she also receives a yearly pension of $203,700. The former president also receives money for office space, supplies, and staff.

PRESIDENTS AND THEIR TERMS

PRESIDENT	PARTY	TOOK OFFICE	LEFT OFFICE	TERMS SERVED	VICE PRESIDENT
George Washington	None	April 30, 1789	March 4, 1797	Two	John Adams
John Adams	Federalist	March 4, 1797	March 4, 1801	One	Thomas Jefferson
Thomas Jefferson	Democratic-Republican	March 4, 1801	March 4, 1809	Two	Aaron Burr, George Clinton
James Madison	Democratic-Republican	March 4, 1809	March 4, 1817	Two	George Clinton, Elbridge Gerry
James Monroe	Democratic-Republican	March 4, 1817	March 4, 1825	Two	Daniel D. Tompkins
John Quincy Adams	Democratic-Republican	March 4, 1825	March 4, 1829	One	John C. Calhoun
Andrew Jackson	Democrat	March 4, 1829	March 4, 1837	Two	John C. Calhoun, Martin Van Buren
Martin Van Buren	Democrat	March 4, 1837	March 4, 1841	One	Richard M. Johnson
William H. Harrison	Whig	March 4, 1841	April 4, 1841	Died During First Term	John Tyler
John Tyler	Whig	April 6, 1841	March 4, 1845	Completed Harrison's Term	Office Vacant
James K. Polk	Democrat	March 4, 1845	March 4, 1849	One	George M. Dallas
Zachary Taylor	Whig	March 5, 1849	July 9, 1850	Died During First Term	Millard Fillmore

PRESIDENT	PARTY	TOOK OFFICE	LEFT OFFICE	TERMS SERVED	VICE PRESIDENT
Millard Fillmore	Whig	July 10, 1850	March 4, 1853	Completed Taylor's Term	Office Vacant
Franklin Pierce	Democrat	March 4, 1853	March 4, 1857	One	William R.D. King
James Buchanan	Democrat	March 4, 1857	March 4, 1861	One	John C. Breckinridge
Abraham Lincoln	Republican	March 4, 1861	April 15, 1865	Served One Term, Died During Second Term	Hannibal Hamlin, Andrew Johnson
Andrew Johnson	Democrat	April 15, 1865	March 4, 1869	Completed Lincoln's Second Term	Office Vacant
Ulysses S. Grant	Republican	March 4, 1869	March 4, 1877	Two	Schuyler Colfax, Henry Wilson
Rutherford B. Hayes	Republican	March 3, 1877	March 4, 1881	One	William A. Wheeler
James A. Garfield	Republican	March 4, 1881	September 19, 1881	Died During First Term	Chester Arthur
Chester Arthur	Republican	September 20, 1881	March 4, 1885	Completed Garfield's Term	Office Vacant
Grover Cleveland	Democrat	March 4, 1885	March 4, 1889	One	Thomas A. Hendricks
Benjamin Harrison	Republican	March 4, 1889	March 4, 1893	One	Levi P. Morton
Grover Cleveland	Democrat	March 4, 1893	March 4, 1897	One	Adlai E. Stevenson
William McKinley	Republican	March 4, 1897	September 14, 1901	Served One Term, Died During Second Term	Garret A. Hobart, Theodore Roosevelt

PRESIDENT	PARTY	TOOK OFFICE	LEFT OFFICE	TERMS SERVED	VICE PRESIDENT
Theodore Roosevelt	Republican	September 14, 1901	March 4, 1909	Completed McKinley's Second Term, Served One Term	Office Vacant, Charles Fairbanks
William Taft	Republican	March 4, 1909	March 4, 1913	One	James S. Sherman
Woodrow Wilson	Democrat	March 4, 1913	March 4, 1921	Two	Thomas R. Marshall
Warren G. Harding	Republican	March 4, 1921	August 2, 1923	Died During First Term	Calvin Coolidge
Calvin Coolidge	Republican	August 3, 1923	March 4, 1929	Completed Harding's Term, Served One Term	Office Vacant, Charles Dawes
Herbert Hoover	Republican	March 4, 1929	March 4, 1933	One	Charles Curtis
Franklin D. Roosevelt	Democrat	March 4, 1933	April 12, 1945	Served Three Terms, Died During Fourth Term	John Nance Garner, Henry A. Wallace, Harry S. Truman
Harry S. Truman	Democrat	April 12, 1945	January 20, 1953	Completed Roosevelt's Fourth Term, Served One Term	Office Vacant, Alben Barkley
Dwight D. Eisenhower	Republican	January 20, 1953	January 20, 1961	Two	Richard Nixon
John F. Kennedy	Democrat	January 20, 1961	November 22, 1963	Died During First Term	Lyndon B. Johnson
Lyndon B. Johnson	Democrat	November 22, 1963	January 20, 1969	Completed Kennedy's Term, Served One Term	Office Vacant, Hubert H. Humphrey
Richard Nixon	Republican	January 20, 1969	August 9, 1974	Completed First Term, Resigned During Second Term	Spiro T. Agnew, Gerald Ford

PRESIDENT	PARTY	TOOK OFFICE	LEFT OFFICE	TERMS SERVED	VICE PRESIDENT
Gerald Ford	Republican	August 9, 1974	January 20, 1977	Completed Nixon's Second Term	Nelson A. Rockefeller
Jimmy Carter	Democrat	January 20, 1977	January 20, 1981	One	Walter Mondale
Ronald Reagan	Republican	January 20, 1981	January 20, 1989	Two	George H.W. Bush
George H.W. Bush	Republican	January 20, 1989	January 20, 1993	One	Dan Quayle
Bill Clinton	Democrat	January 20, 1993	January 20, 2001	Two	Al Gore
George W. Bush	Republican	January 20, 2001	January 20, 2009	Two	Dick Cheney
Barack Obama	Democrat	January 20, 2009	January 20, 2017	Two	Joe Biden

"The imperative need of this nation at all times is the leadership of Uncommon Men or Women." Herbert Hoover

★ WRITE TO THE PRESIDENT ★

You may write to the president at:
The White House
1600 Pennsylvania Avenue NW
Washington, DC 20500

You may e-mail the president at:
comments@whitehouse.gov

Glossary

administrator—a person whose job is to manage an operation, a department, or an office.

challenging (CHA-luhn-jihng)—testing one's strengths or abilities.

debt—something owed to someone else, especially money.

Democrat—a member of the Democratic political party.

development—land that has been modified for a particular use.

economy—the way that a country produces, sells, and buys goods and services.

engineering (ehn-juh-NIHR-ihng)—applying scientific knowledge to a practical purpose such as building machines or buildings.

geology (jee-AH-luh-jee)—the study of the earth and how layers of land were formed.

Great Depression—the period from 1929 to 1942 of worldwide economic trouble. There was little buying and selling, and many people could not find work.

mineral—a natural substance that makes up rocks and other parts of nature.

organization—a group that is put together to accomplish a particular goal.

program—a plan for doing something.

recession (rih-SEH-shuhn)—a period of economic trouble. There is less buying and selling and people may be out of work.

relief—assistance given to those in need.

Republican—a member of the Republican political party.

secretary of commerce—a member of the president's cabinet who is in charge of the Department of Commerce. This department manages the nation's economic development.

stock market—a place where stocks and bonds, which represent parts of businesses, are bought and sold.

World War I—a war fought in Europe from 1914 to 1918.

World War II—a war fought in Europe, Asia, and Africa from 1939 to 1945.

WEBSITES

To learn more about the US Presidents, visit **booklinks.abdopublishing.com**. These links are routinely monitored and updated to provide the most current information available.

Index